HE DOESN'T LOVE YOU IF...

10 Signs He's Not Serious About You & Is Wasting Your Time

KRYSTLE LAUGHTER

He Doesn't Love You If...
10 Signs He's Not Serious About You & Is Wasting Your Time

Krystle Laughter, LLC
Tacoma, WA 98409

Printed in the United States of America

Cover & Interior Design by Krystle Laughter

ISBN
978-1-955787-90-1

CONTENTS

INTRODUCTION

I have wasted years in toxic, dead-end relationships - listening to a man's words while ignoring his actions. At the time, I didn’t realize that a man's actions told me everything I needed to know about him and how he felt about me. You're NOT crazy! You're not asking for too much because you want a man's time, commitment, and full attention. You deserve a man who doesn’t just say that he wants you but shows you he wants you. Let this book educate you, inform you, and be your guide so that you can stop wasting time and have the real love you truly desire.

HE DOESN'T LOVE YOU IF...

YOU HAVE TO CHASE HIM

A woman should never chase a man. I don't care what you've heard. I don't care what you've seen. I don't care what someone told you. A woman who chases a man will never get the man she's chasing. He may date her. He may sleep with her. He may even marry her, but she will never truly have his heart.

She will only be a temporary placeholder until he finds the woman he really wants. I know it sounds harsh but, if you want to be successful in love, you have to be willing to hear and accept the truth. It's the lies that we tell ourselves that get us into the most trouble.

Trying to persuade a man that you're worth his time is the wrong move, Sis. You must know your worth coming into the relationship. If you truly knew your worth, you wouldn't chase a man. You would know that you're worthy of a man who pursues you. You would know that you deserve someone who loves you so much that he'll never allow you to be confused about where he stands with you.

Another thing you must understand about men is that they have an unfair advantage. They typically come into the dating world with more knowledge and experience than women. They are also less emotional which allows them to navigate relationships with foresight and without getting emotionally attached, unlike women. Men decide rather quickly what role you will play in their lives.

This is determined by the man's first impression of you - how you carry yourself and what he thinks you're willing to accept. If you think this sounds unfair, it is. But instead of being upset about it, use it to your advantage. Knowledge is power!

Men are very different from women, but society and some individuals would have you believe that men and women are the same. Not true! All you have to do is stop and look around to discover that men and women are nothing alike. Men are wired to chase women. For a man, the thrill is in the chase.

This is why a man can never love a woman who chases him. A man needs to work for you in order to value you. If you move too quickly, it shows him that you don't value yourself which makes him believe that you're not worth his time. Think about it. Do you value things you don't work for?

Imagine applying for your dream job. It comes with full benefits, six weeks of paid vacation every year, and an amazing retirement plan. You call to inquire about where to send your resume but, before you can even ask, they tell you the job is yours. You are shocked because you know how valuable the job is. You also know that anyone in their right mind wouldn't give something so valuable to someone who they don't even know is qualified for the position. You're excited but, somewhere in the back of your head, you're wondering what the catch is.

This is the same way men approach relationships. If you give a man everything that he wants with him having to do little to nothing to earn it, it tells him that you don't value yourself. A man wants to feel like he has won; like he has gotten something valuable.

He will only feel this way if he has to earn your time, respect, love, and attention. Don't give yourself away freely to a man who hasn't proven his worth just so you can have the relationship. Remember, your worth is not tied to a relationship. You aren't less valuable if you're single. Society lied to you. Stop believing the lies. Now there's nothing wrong with wanting a relationship, but problems arise when you're willing to settle for less just to be in one.

Many women chase men who aren't even worthy of them because the women don't know their worth and are afraid of being alone. Most people don't know how to have a relationship with others because they never learned how to have a healthy relationship with themselves. It's time to heal. A great relationship is waiting for you with a man who will value you. The key is learning to value yourself first.

LESSON #1

Never entertain a relationship with a man you have to chase. You won't have to pursue a man who is really interested in you because he will do the pursuing. If you have to pursue a man, the relationship isn't real. He's most likely dating other women besides you. A man that loves or wants you will never stop chasing you.

THINK IT THROUGH

Have I ever chased a man? Did it work out for me? Do I think I'm worthy of being pursued? Why?

NOTES:

NOTES:

THE MAN FOR YOU
WILL CHASE YOU.

2

HE DOESN'T LOVE YOU IF...

HE DOESN'T COMMUNICATE

Communication is to a relationship what oxygen is to the body; without it, the relationship dies. If you want to know if a man really loves you, look at how he communicates with you. Is he inconsistent? Do you reach out to him more than he reaches out to you? A man who wants to be with you will communicate with you. Women are communicators. Men know this. If a man does not communicate with you or is on and off, or inconsistent, it's intentional.

Why would a man do that? Why would a man intentionally be inconsistent? Well, men like having options the same way a person at a buffet likes the variety.

Be sure of this, a man who is inconsistent in his communication isn't serious about you. He simply wants to keep his options open. He knows that this confusion will keep you stuck. You being stuck means that you won't have the freedom to entertain other men who want to pursue you. Communication is the language of love.

The more you communicate with someone, the more you get to know them and the easier it is for you to fall in love with them. Men who don't communicate with you are not interested in love. They're only interested in one thing: S-E-X. You may not want to believe this, but it's the truth. Never be with a man who doesn't consistently communicate with you. At the least, it's extremely selfish and disrespectful.

At worst, he's dating other women, which is dangerous because you could end up pregnant by a man who will not commit to you or with an incurable disease. It's not worth it. You deserve the best that there is. Someone who doesn't communicate with you does not love you or want you.

LESSON #2

Never settle for a man who is inconsistent in his communication with you. Someone who loves you will take time to learn how to effectively communicate with the woman he cares about. He will communicate with you because he wants you to know that he values you and that you're important to him.

THINK IT THROUGH

Is he consistent with his communication? Does he ghost me? Is this the way I deserve to be treated? Do I deserve better?

NOTES:

NOTES:

THE MAN
FOR YOU WILL
COMMUNICATE
WITH YOU
BECAUSE YOU
MATTER TO HIM.

HE DOESN'T LOVE YOU IF...

He Doesn't Protect You

Men protect things that they love. Ask any man and he will tell you. A man who loves you will protect you physically and emotionally. When you're out in public, he will be watchful to make sure that he's ready to protect you from any outward attacks. When you're around others, he will not allow them to speak negatively about you or disrespect you. When he sees that you are upset, he will do all that he can to make you feel better. Why? He wants to protect your heart.

When a man loves a woman, he doesn't want to do anything to hurt her.

If a man tells you that he loves you but constantly causes you physical or emotional pain, he is lying to you. Granted, no one is perfect and everyone has bad days - but a man who is consistently rude, inconsiderate, and hurtful doesn't care about you. Never stay with a man who is comfortable breaking your heart.

The man that is for you will protect your heart. He will watch you and learn from you. He will find joy in making you happy. The things that are important to you will be important to him as well. You will feel safe and secure in his arms. He will be trustworthy. You won't have to wonder if someone else has his heart because he will show you that his heart belongs only to you.

Another way a man who loves you protects your heart will be by not entertaining close relationships with other women who are not family members.

When a man loves you, he will cut off relationships with other women because he will not want to take a chance on it being a temptation for him. He will also not want to make you feel insecure or unsure in any way. He will want to build with you. You will become his best female friend.

Any man who maintains relationships with other women other than family members is playing games with you. Cut him off because you cannot trust him.

LESSON #3

A real man is not afraid to protect the women he loves. He will confront people who dishonor you because you are important to him. He will cut off non-relative female friendships.

THINK IT THROUGH

Do I feel protected? How do I feel? Is this how I want to feel for the rest of my life?

NOTES:

NOTES:

THE MAN FOR YOU WILL PROTECT YOU.

HE DOESN'T LOVE YOU IF...

HE DOESN'T RESPECT YOU

For men, respect equals love. If a man doesn't show you respect, there's no way that he can love you. I will say it again, women fail to understand that men and women are different. It's this ignorance that causes men to continue to have the upper hand in relationships. All you have to do is look around to see it: men juggling multiple women - men with jobs and men without jobs, good-looking men and unattractive men.

It's not hard for a man to get women because most women get their identity from their relationships and don't know their worth.

That's how a below-average man can get a good-looking woman. That's how a man with nothing going for himself gets a smart woman with a degree, a good job, and a house. Men are not stupid when it comes to dating and women. They are very careful and calculated. The reason it is so important for us women to understand men is so that we can differentiate between good men and men who just want to play games.

The truth is, some men will play with your body but never do what it takes to earn your heart. This is why you must gain the knowledge to protect yourself from people with bad intentions. I know this is hard to hear, but a wise person once told me: "The truth hurts, but then it heals you".

In order for a man to respect you, you must first respect yourself. What does that look like? Self-respect means that you know your worth.

You don’t settle for poor treatment or leftovers. You know what you deserve and you're not afraid to ask for it. A woman who respects herself is not afraid to let go of people who dishonor her.

A woman who knows her worth also respects herself in the way she dresses. She is sexy, yet classy at the same time. She doesn’t expose her entire body for the world to see. Women don't even respect other women who do that. It sends the message that a woman is trying to get attention. This usually attracts the wrong type of attention. When you respect yourself, it shows in how you dress and demonstrates the love you have for yourself. Self-love equals self-respect.

Men respect women they love because their behavior demands respect.

If a man does not show you respect in the way he treats you and talks to you, he doesn't love you. You shouldn’t want this man either. Love someone who loves you. There is someone for you who will love and respect you.

LESSON #4

Never allow a man to disrespect you. The man who wants you will respect you because he knows that without respect there is no love. Remember, love equals respect for a man. A man who doesn't honor your boundaries, time, or wishes is disrespectful and shouldn't be tolerated. You have to start seeing yourself as the prize you are. When you do, you won't settle for less.

THINK IT THROUGH

Is respect important to me? What does respect look like? What does respect feel like?

NOTES:

THE MAN FOR YOU WILL RESPECT YOU.

HE DOESN'T LOVE YOU IF...

HE CONFUSES YOU

Many women are confused about their relationships because the men they are with give them mixed signals. A man who loves you will never do this because he wants you to know how he feels about you. A man who loves you will never confuse you because he doesn't want to lose you. He will call you. He will spend his time with you. A man who is just there to play games with you doesn't want you to have clarity about the relationship because clarity means that you know he's not serious about you.

Men who play games with women want to leave them confused so that they don't have time to weigh their options. They will drag you along for months or even years because they know that you will wait as long as it takes for him to give you an answer. Boy, bye! Real men know what they want. If you're dealing with someone who is confusing you, run! It's intentional. Someone who cares about you would never intentionally confuse you.

You must love yourself enough to let go of people who don't have your best interest at heart. Stop wasting your time waiting and hoping for someone to love you. You must learn to love yourself. I know these lessons are hard, but you've already been through so much. You deserve better. Better to be hurt over the truth, than to be hurt by lies and continue to get your heart broke. Let this truth hurt you, so that afterward it can heal you.

LESSON #5

A man who loves you will provide you with clarity because he wants you to know how he feels about you. He won't allow you to be confused about the relationship because he doesn't want to risk losing you. A man who allows you to be confused doesn't care about you. He is concerned with getting what he wants, and he will break your heart if you stay with him.

THINK IT THROUGH

What does confusion look like? How should a healthy relationship make me feel?

NOTES:

THE MAN FOR YOU WON'T CONFUSE YOU.

HE DOESN'T LOVE YOU IF...

HE ABUSES YOU

A mentor of mine says, love speaks many languages - and abuse is not one of them. If a man is abusing you in any way, shape, or form, he doesn't love you. Let me be clear on this! A man who loves you will never abuse you. Think about yourself. How do you treat the people you love? Do you ever think about hurting them in any way?

When it comes to relationships, women lead with their hearts. We must instead learn to lead with our heads first and then our hearts. I know this seems contrary to intuition, but you must approach love logically if you ever want to win.

Don't fall in love, walk in love. Falling in love is accidental because people don't usually fall on purpose. Walking in love is intentional. It means taking your time to get to know someone, their personality, and whether they are truly a good fit for you.

Falling in love is risky because you could end up with a heartbreaker, an abuser, or an emotionally unavailable partner. By the time you discover who the man truly is, it will be too late because your heart is already involved. Being intentional about love by learning to walk in love will protect you.

Like I stated before, love and abuse do not go together. If you're being abused physically, mentally, emotionally, financially, or spiritually, you need to find a way out. I know it's easier said than done, but you deserve a healthy relationship with a healthy person.

An intimate relationship should make you feel safe and secure, not afraid. If the man you're with makes you feel afraid or you have to walk on eggshells when you're around him, it's not a healthy relationship.

A man who loves you will want you to be yourself. He will embrace all your quirkiness and uniqueness and it will be special to him because it's what makes you, you. He will not belittle you or put you down for being different or having imperfections. You cannot thrive in an abusive relationship because abuse is built on control and domination.

You were meant to live free. You deserve better, Sis! Please understand that you are worth so much more. Love yourself first and let that relationship go!

LESSON #6

A man who loves you will never abuse you because abuse is the opposite of love. A man may say he loves you and even occasionally act like it but, if he abuses you in any form, he doesn't love you. A man will never abuse the women he loves because men protect things they love.

THINK IT THROUGH

Can someone love you and still abuse you?

Why or why not?

NOTES:

NOTES:

THE MAN FOR YOU

WILL NEVER

ABUSE YOU.

HE DOESN'T LOVE YOU IF...

HE WASTES YOUR TIME

Time is one of the most precious resources we have, and men know this. A grown boy will tell you he's going to call you and not do it. He will make a date and then cancel at the last minute. He will call you and text you at all hours of the night because that's what he wants to do. He will always consider himself before you; you will never be his priority. A man who wastes your time doesn't love you.

The moment a man starts treating you like an option instead of a priority, you need to do the same to him. If he respects you and really wants you, he'll change his behavior.

If he's just there to play games, he'll ignore you and expect you to chase him. Give him the shock of his life and let him go! You are a queen, and queens don't chase men.

Real men respect women. Respecting a woman means respecting her time. It means treating her the same way he wants to be treated, with the hopes that she will reciprocate.

Never play around with a man who doesn't respect time because this means that he doesn't respect himself. A man that doesn't respect himself lacks self-love. And a man who doesn't love himself is incapable of loving anyone else.

Additionally, a man who loves you wants to build with you. Building a relationship with someone takes time. A man who is really into you wants to get to know you by spending time with you. Remember, for men, the joy is in the chase. His greatest pleasure will be hearing you talk, seeing your face, and knowing that you're happy just being in his presence.

Stay away from men who claim to never have time for you. He will use his responsibilities and obligations as an excuse as to why he doesn't have time for you. We all have lives. A man shouldn't be with you if he doesn't have time. You need someone who is willing and available to meet your needs. That's not too much to ask for; that's just relationship basics. Level-up your standards, Sis. You're worth it.

Lesson #7

A man who loves you won't waste your time because he knows your time is valuable. Real men respect the women they love and this includes their time. A man who isn't concerned with wasting your time won't be concerned with protecting your heart, and that's unacceptable.

THINK IT THROUGH

Do I value my own time? Do I expect others to value my time?

NOTES:

NOTES:

THE MAN FOR YOU WON'T WASTE YOUR TIME, BECAUSE HE'LL BE BUSY SPENDING TIME WITH YOU!

HE DOESN'T LOVE YOU IF...

HE'S UNFAITHFUL

A man who loves you will be faithful to you. Everybody makes mistakes, but let's be real: do you really want to be with someone who's comfortable making those types of mistakes? It could cost you your health, or worse, your life. Incurable sexually transmitted diseases are real! Are you okay with your partner sleeping with other women and then coming back home and sleeping with you? Well, that's what happens when your partner is unfaithful. Do you really want to live knowing that your spouse could have gotten another woman pregnant and never told you? These are all possible scenarios when you accept an unfaithful partner.

Is it fair that the man who says he loves you and expects you to be faithful, doesn't love you enough to be faithful to you? I don't know about you, but to me that's unacceptable. As women, we must learn to love ourselves more. Having a warm body next to you doesn't equal a real relationship. There is someone for you who will be faithful to you and only have eyes for you!

A man who is unfaithful lacks self-control. Mature men and women understand that self-control is an essential part of adulthood. This is why you don't see most adults going around throwing temper tantrums and hitting people. That's what children do. The kind of man that you want to be in a relationship with will learn how to discipline himself and not put himself in tempting situations. He will also have nothing to hide. Be wary of a man that can't set his phone down in your presence. That's a sign that he's hiding something. A relationship requires trust, but trust must be earned. Don't give it away too quickly. Let him earn it, slowly, over time.

A man shouldn't be emotionally unfaithful either. He shouldn't be confiding in other women; that's emotional cheating and a red flag. This includes people in places of authority such as female leaders, bosses, pastors, etc. In a relationship, a man should discuss any relationship issues he has with his partner. Anything that is shared about your relationship outside of the two of you, should be agreed upon between both of you, and with both parties present.

Don't let a man make you doubt your intuition in this area. If you feel as though he is being unfaithful or is participating in an inappropriate relationship with another woman, trust your gut. A woman's intuition is very powerful and usually accurate. If your senses are telling you that he is lying, hiding something, or being unfaithful, believe it and move accordingly.

Never beg a man to be faithful to you. You are not a dog. You are a queen, and queens don't beg.

LESSON #8

A man who loves you will be faithful to you. He knows faithfulness is required to maintain a healthy and lasting relationship and won't do anything to jeopardize it. Never stay with a man who is unfaithful to you because he doesn't respect you or your commitment to him. This is a sign of poor character, and that's not someone you want to spend your life with. You deserve someone who is faithful, trustworthy, and has integrity.

THINK IT THROUGH

Do you believe faithful men exist? Do you believe you deserve a faithful man?

NOTES:

THE MAN FOR YOU

WILL BE

FAITHFUL.

HE DOESN'T LOVE YOU IF...

HE MAKES EXCUSES INSTEAD OF CHANGES

A man who loves you won't make excuses, he'll make changes. A real man expects his woman to hold him to a certain level of behavior. He loves her because she makes him a better man. The two hold each other accountable, and they grow together. On the other hand, grown boys have no desire to be held accountable. Instead, they will make excuses, tell you that all men are this way, or give you excuses for why they don't keep their word.

If a man tells you he's going to do something and he doesn't do it, that's a red flag. Relationships are built on trust. Real men know that if they don't keep their word, you won't be able to trust them. A grown boy is hoping that he can break his promise to you with little to no consequence because this enablement tells him that you don't love yourself. A grown boy loves this type of woman because he knows that he can lie to her, cheat on her, and maybe even abuse her and she won't leave him.

A man who doesn't respect you is a dangerous man. Never let a man disrespect you twice! This is how women end up in abusive relationships. The signs were always there, you just missed them. You're a queen, and you deserve a king.

If you want love, you must learn to love and accept yourself first. I talk about this in more detail in my book: Love Yourself First:

How to Heal from Toxic People, Create Healthy Relationships & Become a Confident Woman. You must hold a man accountable; otherwise, he will walk all over you. You have to show him that you know who you are and that you will not tolerate disrespect or inconsistency. You don't demand this with words. You demand it with actions!

If a man does something you don't like one time, you need to let him know in a firm, calm, and unemotional manner; that's the first warning. If he continues to repeat this behavior, you must leave him immediately. No discussions, arguments, no ifs, ands, or buts.

LESSON #9

A man who loves you won't make excuses, he'll make changes. A man who is stubborn and unwilling to change doesn't love you. There is no love without sacrifice. You can't have a healthy relationship with someone who is not interested in changing the things that hinder or hurt the relationship. Relationships take two people working together and being considerate of the other. If someone does not want to do this, don't waste your time?

THINK IT THROUGH

Is love worth changing for? Should we change for the people we love? Why?

NOTES:

NOTES:

THE MAN FOR YOU
WON'T MAKE
EXCUSES,
HE'LL MAKE
CHANGES.

HE DOESN'T LOVE YOU IF...

YOU HAVE TO ASK

When you are loved you don't have to ask because love is seen and felt before it's heard. Read that again. Love is seen and felt long before it's ever heard. This is how a baby understands the love given to him by his mother. He can't communicate it with words, but he smiles, coo's, and laughs. His body language tells the story of safety, satisfaction, and security. He feels loved. Likewise, the love of a man is felt by the woman he loves. It's seen in her smile, her laugh, her peace, and her joy.

If you have to wonder if a man loves you, he probably doesn't. Love cannot be hidden. Real love speaks for itself. When a man loves you, the whole world will know. It will be evident in the way he speaks to you, the way he treats you, the way he talks about you. Don't be fooled. A man who loves you will let you know with his actions and his words. Run from any man who says he loves you but doesn't show it. He's lying. Always believe actions over words.

Never want someone so badly that you're willing to compromise your self-love and self-respect to be with him. Any man who is comfortable with you losing your identity isn't worth having. If you are compromising your self-respect to be with a man, you need to pause and figure out why you stopped loving yourself. What happened to you? Who hurt you?

Who told you you weren't good enough to

have a whole man? Go back to that place and space and reclaim your power. You are not what someone did to you. You are not what people said about you. You're not even what you believe about yourself: YOU ARE SO MUCH MORE. You are worthy. You are valuable. You are loved! Never forget that.

LESSON #10

If you have to wonder if a man loves you, the answer is probably “no”. When a man loves you, it will be evident to all - especially the woman he loves. A man will show you how he feels about you with his actions. When his actions don’t line up with his words, always believe his actions.

THINK IT THROUGH

What does my gut tell me about my relationship? Do his words match his actions?

NOTES:

THE MAN FOR YOU WILL SHOW YOU THAT HE LOVES YOU AS WELL AS TELL YOU.

APOLOGIZE TO YOURSELF

It's very important that you apologize to yourself for all of the things you've settled for. It's time to heal. Forgive yourself for every relationship you had with someone who didn't deserve you or value you. Forgive yourself for allowing people to treat you like an option instead of a priority. Forgive yourself for treating others better than you treat yourself. Apologize to yourself for the time you've wasted. Tell yourself "sorry", for every tear you've had to cry. Forgive yourself for ignoring your intuition.

Apologize to yourself for not listening to people who tried to warn you. Forgive yourself because we all make mistakes. Just don't let your mistakes make you. Learn the lessons, so that you don't repeat them. Learn how to love yourself. Learn how to be good to you. When you learn how to be good to yourself, then you begin to expect that same treatment from others.

You cannot wait until someone abuses you or cheats on you to know that you won't tolerate this type of behavior. You need to know this before entering into a relationship. That's what having standards and boundaries are for. If you set standards and boundaries before entering into a relationship, you will avoid relationships that devalue you and that you were never supposed to be in.

Your desires, your values, your boundaries, and your standards are important. You deserve to be with someone who sees you as important too. Never settle for a relationship, even if that means being alone. It's better to be alone than to be miserable. You deserve better than that!

Rise up and be the queen you were called to be. Stop accepting trash when you were made to have treasure. Work on yourself and become the woman of your own dreams. Build your business, build your self-confidence, know your worth and go from there. I love you, and I'm rooting for you, Girl!

A LETTER TO YOURSELF

Write a letter to yourself. In this letter, I want you to ask yourself for forgiveness. Write down your personal standards and boundaries. I want you to write out your dreams and goals. Write the ways you will improve your mind, body, and spirit. I'm proud of the work that you are doing. Don't stop. This is just the beginning. Read more books, listen to podcasts, and keep going, glowing and growing.

MY LETTER:

ABOUT THE AUTHOR

Krystle Laughter is an author, mentor, consultant and speaker from Seattle, Washington. Her passion is to empower and educate women. She utilizes her platforms to uplift women - encouraging them to heal from toxic relationships, to develop self-love, and to become authors so that their stories may change lives as well. She is the creator of Krystle Laughter Academy and has authored numerous books including the Love Yourself Series, as well as many children's books. To learn more, follow her on social media and visit krystlelaughter.org.

WHAT TO READ NEXT

If this book opened your eyes to unhealthy relationship patterns, the next step is rebuilding your self-worth and standards so you never settle for less again.
Start with these books from Krystle Laughter:

Love Yourself First
Learn how to heal from toxic relationships, rebuild self-confidence, and understand your true value.

Love Yourself Again
Discover how to create strong boundaries, stop being a doormat, and develop the confidence to demand healthier relationships.

Love Yourself First Workbook
Put the lessons into practice with guided exercises designed to help you apply self-love, boundaries, and personal growth to your life.

OTHER BOOKS

LOVE YOURSELF FIRST

Healing begins with the relationship you have with yourself. In Love Yourself First, Krystle Laughter helps women break free from toxic relationship patterns, rebuild self-worth, and learn the power of self-love. This empowering guide will help you recognize your value, stop settling for less, and start choosing relationships that truly honor you.

LOVE YOURSELF AGAIN

If you've ever struggled with people-pleasing, weak boundaries, or accepting less than you deserve, this book will help you reclaim your power. Love Yourself Again teaches women how to stop being a doormat, create strong personal standards, and develop the confidence to demand healthier relationships. It's time to rebuild your boundaries and choose yourself again.

LOVE YOURSELF FIRST: KIDS

Love Yourself First Kids teaches children the foundations of confidence, kindness, and self-love in a fun and easy-to-understand way. Through simple lessons and colorful characters, kids learn how to value themselves, treat others with respect, and build healthy self-esteem from an early age. A powerful message for young hearts and growing minds.

LOVE YOURSELF FIRST: AFFIRMATION JOURNAL

Transform the way you speak to yourself. This journal contains 100 powerful affirmations designed to help women build confidence, establish healthy boundaries, heal emotionally, and embrace self-worth. By practicing these affirmations daily, you'll strengthen your mindset and begin showing up in life and relationships with greater confidence and clarity.

LOVE YOURSELF FIRST: THE WORKBOOK

Take the lessons from Love Yourself First to the next level with this interactive workbook. Each section walks you through deeper reflection, exercises, and guided prompts designed to help you apply the principles of self-love, healing, and personal growth to your own life. It's a practical step-by-step companion for women ready to do the inner work and create lasting change.

Krystle Laughter Academy

Ready to take your healing and personal growth even further?

Krystle Laughter Academy is an online learning platform designed to help women heal from toxic relationships, rebuild self-confidence, and create healthier standards for their lives and relationships.

Visit KrystleLaughterAcademy.com to explore courses, tools, and resources designed to help you grow, heal, and thrive.

www.ingramcontent.com/pod-product-compliance
Lightning Source LLC
LaVergne TN
LVHW010936110826
845149LV00013B/2621

* 9 7 8 1 9 5 5 7 8 7 9 1 8 *